The Push
The Pull
And the Prayer

LaToya K Bilbo

The Push The Pull and The Prayer

Copyright © 2015 LaToya K Bilbo
Kingdom Builders Publications

All rights reserved. No part of this book may be reproduced or transmitted in any form or by any means without written permission from the author.

ISBN: 978-0-69253-346-8
Library of Congress Control Number: 2015952266
Photography – LH "Just Pose" Photography

Cover Designer – Mark Linen Kwonyah Designs
 LoMar Designs

Editors: Kingdom Builders Publication Staff
Nichole Smith
Louise James

Printed in USA
Go to our website: www.kingdombuilderspublications.com

Kingdom Builders Publications LLC

DEDICATION

I would like to give honor to my Savior, Jesus! I am so glad He created me in His image and likeness, and put His gifts in me to write, encourage, and minister to others about His goodness. I thank God for opening doors for me throughout my journey, allow me to talk about personal trials, tribulations, and testimonies out of love. I thank God in advance for the lives touched by the writings prior and present books, and those to follow.

I thank my husband, Theodore Bilbo Jr. whom I affectionately call Mister B. You are an awesome encouragement. Baby, you support my dreams and ambitions. I truly love and thank you for being my husband and soul mate.

I dedicate this book to my firstborn miracle Tijah N. Kennedy, second born Titus Theodore Bilbo (deceased) and my miracle Liberty L. I. Bilbo. Wallace & Bethsheba Kennedy, Airrion Kennedy, Natasha Simmons and family, Ella M. Bilbo, Theodore Bilbo Sr., Michelle Walser, Ernest & Cynthia Jones and Latonia Bilbo.

I thank God for my sister in Christ, Melinda Heyward. When we first met, it was not our season but as time progressed, God revealed his perfect timing for us. Once this book releases, you will be married to the man God sent just for you and I am honored to be included in your special day. I thank God for my sister in Christ Helen Bishop. Girl, you had no idea that God sent you into my life as an angel, and that one moment has changed my entire life. I am so grateful for you and your kindhearted spirit. I am thankful God allowed our paths to cross again, because He knew exactly what we needed. I thank God for my mentor and spiritual leader Stephanie Kirkland. The class "In Pursuit of Me" couldn't have come at a better time in my life. God wanted me to transition into a new creature, but I didn't want to leave the old me. I fought against the pricks to shift but when I saw "It's Time" written on your description of the course, I was convinced that it was for me. God told me at the beginning of that year "it's time" and I knew He was confirming His voice to me. Through your ministry, I've truly developed as a woman of God. My Noah word was formed: "Restoration" with subtitles: "New Beginnings and Fresh Start." I am ready to affect lives. I thank my "In Pursuit of Me" accountability partner LaQuetia L. Gilliard, who was much more. The power of your love is immeasurable. To my friend and sister in Christ, Prophetess Terressa Weston you have influenced my life with your free spirit, obedience, eagle soaring character, and personality. I am so glad that our paths crossed. I know there is so much more ahead. A special thank you to Pastors Sandra and J Lionel Williams; you both exemplify awesome worship, and serving God in excellence is your name. I love you both to life! Greater things are ahead for you and the ministry you lead.

You didn't know me personally, I saw a flyer inviting people to come worship with you all and because of that experience, God has joined us in spirit and life. To my sister in Christ Annette W. Austin, a special thanks to you woman of God; for when I lost my son Titus, you sent me a personal letter of your story and some other materials to read even though you didn't know me. You will never know the impact you made to my soul and spirit.

Thank God, for you and I pray that God will manifest in your life as He has done in mine. I would be remiss if I did not mention these two special women. We spent more time than with our own families during the workweek - my sisters Sylvia R. Jones and Maxima Holmes. Ladies, I appreciate you both. We are coworkers and friends. It was not by happenstance the three of us were placed in the office together. I am able to be myself, free and silly, without judgement. We "play" but we will "pray" at a moment's notice. I am also grateful for three women that join me in intercessory prayer, Nicole Mason, Ebony Clark, and Mishelle Waldon. God did not make a mistake. To whom much is given, much is required. Man may change their minds about us, but God has never changed His mind about us. He has called us, ordained us, and predestined us for such a time as this.

Many people have touched and crossed my path. I am grateful to all of you. I pray we will see each other again…if not in this lifetime, then when we go to be with our Father.

I would like to thank Kingdom Builders Publications and Pen of a Ready Writer Society for this awesome opportunity to be a part of the organization and express my writing through your contest. I won in a category that was not even an original category. God stepped in and created a new one for "Inspirational Writing," of which I am so grateful! I must say thank you to Minister Louise Smith for her dedication, encouragement, and PUSH. You were never bugging me, you were pushing me into my destiny, I am grateful.

I send another special thanks to my Pastor, Apostle Renaldo S., and First Lady Tricia Turner for welcoming my family into the ministry with open arms. I remember the first day I walked through the doors of Changing Lives Christian Center which is now "New Destiny Church International." Tuesday nights was Bible study. It seems that evening October 2013 was set-aside just for me. Bible study had been interrupted by an awesome move of God. On the first night of my visit, I went to the altar crying, not caring who was watching. The Pastor prayed and prophesied to the people of God, and the words spoken told my story. Pastor Turner spoke directly to my spirit. My family joined me the following Sunday and we've been there ever since. Thanks for the great teachings you give weekly. I can't wait to see the impact we will have in the nations. I appreciate you both.

This book is dedicated to all the daily email and text readers, Facebook friends and family, and anyone I am connected to whether known or unknown that are reading and being inspired. Thank you all.

CONTENTS

	Dedication	iii
	Foreword	vii
	Introduction	ix
1	In the Beginning	11
2	The First Time	14
3	The Second Time	20
4	The Next Attempt	29
5	In Pursuit of Me	33
6	God Supernaturally Intervenes	39
7	The Process	43
8	Abraham and Sarah	52
9	Wounds and Scars are not a Waste	55
10	Blood Transfusion	58
11	The Pit the Prison and the Palace	60
12	What Can Hinder the Move of God	63
13	Wait on Your Promise	69
	Encouragement and Closing Remarks	71

FOREWORD

This book, THE PUSH, THE PULL, AND THE PRAYER by Latoya Bilbo will certainly spark your life with the power of God. Latoya holds nothing back regarding her journey, which was filled with disappointment, pain, inner struggles, and question that many ask, but never express to anyone. As you read this book, you will quickly see the power of God from beginning to end. Even in the pain, God was always there. I am proud of Latoya for being open enough to write about this very trying journey with God. As I read this book, I could not help but think about the number of women and men who gave up; thought God had forgotten them. This read could empower you to be relentless in faith. Hold on. God will supernaturally intervene. Just as God restored Latoya, certainly He will restore you while you are reading this book. Just when man said it could not and would not happen, I declare that as you read the book, God will supernaturally move upon your life and hope and faith will once again rise up in your spirit.

Finally, there is no substitute for FAITH. Without it, there is no hope. (Hebrews 11:6)

~ Renaldo S. Turner, Pastor
New Destiny Church International

The Push, The Pull, and The Prayer is the story of a journey. It teaches us that victory is available to those who trust God through vicissitudes. It reminds us that not all "deliverance" is instantaneous but all ends in Victory no matter your path, if you position yourself to experience it. The scripture that comes to my heart is *Romans 8:18*. *"The suffering of this present time is not worthy to be compared with the glory that shall be revealed in you."* This lets me know that even when I go through, I gain if I allow God to go through with me. Each stage of our journey has lessons that develop and position us for the Victory. We must be open for the lessons and obedient to Holy Spirit as he gently leads us forward. LaToya's Journey is a beautiful example of learning how to allow Holy Spirit to lead and obeying, which brings LIBERTY. Let her message speak life into your circumstance as you move towards your FREEDOM.

~ *Stephanie M. Kirkland,*
Life Coach CEO/Founder – In Pursuit of Me

Prepare to be catapulted into your destiny as your faith is increased through the testimony and prayer life exemplified by Prophetess LaToya Bilbo. I'm not just making a suggestion for another good book, but I have personally been privileged to witness her testimony of faith. Her life is a true example of "The just shall live by faith!" Her daily posts, texts, and waves of encouragement have helped to push others to where God has called us to in faith. I encourage each reader to open up your Spirit to receive what the Lord desires to release through the penned message of this great vessel of honor.

~ *Sandra Williams,*
Co-Pastor House of Judah Outreach Center

INTRODUCTION

I know there are many people facing different situations in their personal and public lives. Some have given up the fight, forgotten their desires, and turned back, while others have chosen to trust God no matter what. This book is to encourage each of you. You can find yourself going through different seasons in each of these areas of your life, but you have a choice to make. You can choose to be miserable, in doubt, discouraged, down all the time, in a permanent funk, depressed, unhappy, low, rejected, neglected, and disheartened or you can choose to be just the opposite.

We do face times where we may be unhappy about something going on, hurt, disappointed, or even discouraged, but we CANNOT stay there. It is very vital for our destiny not to stay in a place of depression and disappointment because it will rob you of what's ahead through Christ.

I've faced similar times through various stages of life, but I had to make a choice, "God no matter what, even if you don't do this, I know you CAN and I know you are ABLE." It may not take the pain away, but making a righteous decision transforms your thinking.

I am writing my story, praying that somebody will be touched, healed, set free, and delivered. It is my hope that a life will change through the words in this book. My intentions are to shed light on darkness. I will not use real names or places. God never called me to be that type of woman, but tactful, considerate, and sensitive to His Spirit.

As I begin to reveal a part of me to you, you may see yourself or similarities but most of all, I hope you see Christ working through me.

I just want to remind you never put limitations on Christ because He is a BIG God. God will never fail and can turn what may look impossible into "Yes, I did that," all because of his abilities. He can.

I am so grateful for the things God places in me daily to bless others, whether through an email, text, or phone conversation. It's been a while since my freshmen published book. God has been dealing with me to write new books. Although it has taken a moment, I am excited to share this book **THE PUSH, THE PULL AND THE PRAYER** with you. I hope you be will encouraged, inspired, and blessed.

If you have not read the first book, **T.O.O.L. (TRIALS, TRIBULATIONS & TESTIMONIES OUT OF LOVE)**, I encourage you to get a copy and allow God to speak to you through its pages.

I must say that when I began writing this book, it started out as a 40-day devotional, but God shifted what would be written. I had to be obedient to His voice although I was thinking, "I'm getting halfway through and this is where you want me to go?" "Yes." "Wow!" Well you've guessed it; I am moving by His voice and 'The Push, The Pull and The Prayer' will dig deeper into an area of my life I battled with, that was a struggle, a closed closet to visit; quiet place, and a walk of faith.

"All things work together for the good of those that love God and are called according to His purpose." Romans 8:28

Let's embark this journey together. God will lead and let us follow. Amen!

~ LaToya Bilbo

IN THE BEGINNING
Chapter One

In the Beginning...

As a little girl, I imagined myself married with five or six children. I could see the white dress I would wear at my wedding, not really seeing a husband, but the princess dream of every little girl to have a prince charming or knight in shining armor with little patter of feet was my dream life. I had a couple of names chosen for my babies. I would pretend often - drifting away in a fantasy world using my dolls to act out how everything would be.

I would set my dolls and teddy bears up around the room and pretend as if I were a teacher and preacher. I got joy believing my subjects understood what I was saying. Now, you know you enjoyed make believe too. It took you to the greatest place in your thoughts.

I lived in Germany for a brief moment of my childhood and I remember distinctly one Christmas holiday, I sat on Santa Claus's lap. He asked, "What do you want for Christmas little girl?" My reply was, "I want a little brother." Out of all the things I could have asked for, a little brother seemed most important. Well, not long after the request was asked for, the request was granted; and my mom was pregnant with a boy child. She named him Airrion, awesome! Look at God.

As I grew older, my mother did not have more children so I used my sister and brother as my students. Along with my original dolls and teddy bear collection, I would teach, preach or boss them all around. Sometimes I spoke to the walls, in hopes they were paying attention.

In development, I pondered the amount of children I would love to have and it was still five, six, or more. I wanted a big family. My mother was an only child, and my dad has eight other siblings. Both grandparents had large families. I loved the job of babysitting when I became a teen and it continued until I graduated high school. I wanted God to bless me with a house full of my own someday.

If you read my first book, you discovered I could've had a few children along the way based on the lifestyle I lived, but for some reason it didn't really occur to me at the time.

I remember hearing my Dad say, "We better not wind up getting pregnant or else..." That stuck in my head, but I never thought it would happen to me before I was married.

I met Travis (fictional name), and my whole life changed. In the beginning of our relationship, we were becoming acquainted with one another and sex was not an option. As we became more familiar, sex seemed to be the right thing to do because of our love for each other. We started out occasionally using a contraceptive. I certainly could not get on the pill because my parents would find out that I was sexually active, so the only alternative was a condom. After dating for a while, we threw caution to the wind. Our carelessness included no condoms at all. What in the world was I thinking? I wanted children, but I wanted them once I got married. In the moment of love and passion, logic went right out the window. I knew better, but my hormones, who and what I wanted was more important than my relationship with God. It was all about me. I could feel myself becoming addicted to what I desired to have...and that was my boyfriend. At that point, my emotions and soul was wrapped up into him, and that was okay with me. "I loved him." I thought I knew what love was and this had to be love.

I never thought about being pregnant. I was having the time of my life; months of precarious sex with no regards; thinking as an immature person thinks; nothing's going to happen, we were good, most likely nothing would happen. I didn't take a lot of time to think of the consequences of our actions.

There is a TV show called 16 and Pregnant. Recently, while watching this show, I thought what if they had those during my time, would I have thought more?" "Would I have made better decisions?" "Would I have thought twice about what I was doing and what could happen?" I really can't say, but based on the culture of today's tweens and teens, they are still getting pregnant. Boys are still making babies and leaving the mothers to care for the children alone. Mothers are having babies and abandoning their babies while the system or their parents are raising them.

"Are these shows beneficial; are they truly helping?" I believe they are but marginally. When that mindset sets in wanting to be grown and do what the mind wants to do, many times, logic goes right out of the window. We know better, but don't care; we just want what we want!

I want to address our young girls, tweens, teens, and unmarried young adults. Every time you decide to lie between the sheets, giving yourself away, you are making the decision, "Today I want to get pregnant and/or get a disease." Yes, that's right. You are making a conscious unrighteous decision because there is too much information out there today to be making some of the same choices that your parents made, or your grandparents made. If we keep doing the same things expecting different results, it is called insanity but we change the game by making better choices and teaching by examples and with our lives. We can't continue hiding behind who we were or what we did.

Today, we need to be real. I'm not saying you have to reveal every skeleton falling out your closet, but it's time to keep it real. Our daughters and sons are looking to us. If we don't tell them, then the streets will surely show them. Therefore, we have to REACH and TEACH now before EACH one of our babies start having babies of their own, diseases uncured, and unhealthy relationships leading to destruction and abuse.

Everything has a beginning, so today let's begin by really taking life a bit more seriously. As Pastor Turner says, "We should have some non-negotiables in our lives." I will simply not do some things.

THE FIRST TIME
Chapter Two

LaToya has a man, yes I do! I was in college and finally dating, but my choice of a man was not approved by my family because he was a G.I. (Government Issue) soldier. I was enjoying myself and I loved me some him. It didn't start out that way, but that's how it wound up after months of getting to know one another. When we decided to become intimate, I made the choice that getting pregnant or a disease was okay. No, I didn't say that out of my mouth or even think it, but that's what I was doing. Not only was I doing that, I was killing parts of me daily as I continued to live in darkness, in sin. I've been in church majority of my life and I loved being an active member of the body from young until now, but I didn't really know what a real relationship with Christ was. I wanted to live my life and have some fun. Every day I got weaker and weaker in my faith and didn't even know it.

Men, women, teenagers, boys and girls, we lose ourselves when we attach ourselves to sin, to darkness, to things that are not of Christ. When we know to do right and we still do wrong, it's a sin, point blank! We can't say we don't enjoy acts of sin. If that were the case else we wouldn't do it. We enjoyed what we did, but when we know better, we must do better. God is watching us as well as people around us.

After a while, sex became the new norm. As time progressed, without taking proper precautions, the inevitable happened. My relationship with my GI man was falling apart. We had a plethora of misunderstandings but more importantly and fearfully, I missed my period. I told myself, "Okay, I know I am not pregnant, I must be going through menopause." As ridiculous as that sounds for an 18 year old to mention menopause during the most fertile time of life had to be a rhetorical statement. I went to the store to grab a pregnancy test; I was scared out of my mind. My dad's voice kept playing in the back of my head. My man has been stationed to Georgia, I'm in Kansas, and we are having a few issues. Walking through the doors of the house and heading to the bathroom had to be the longest walk of my life. Looking at the instructions and taking out the test, I was shivering in my shoes. This cannot come out positive. I am not pregnant.

Proceeding..................I closed my eyes, opened my eyes, and then I looked down. What I saw next changed my life forever. It was positive. What I thought would not be reality had just become real. Oh my God, all I could do was cry. I wanted a lot of children but not like this. What am I going to do? I can't tell my parents, they will kill me. I will be kicked out of the house. What am I going to do? My dad is going to kill Travis and me, literally. Let me get a subscription now for the daily newspaper, because LaToya is about to hit the headliner.

Well, I figured, I am not showing, so I will just wait. What you do in the dark will eventually expose itself in the light. Some people may not gain weight when they get pregnant, but most people are going to show and you can only hide for so long. The shame, the guilt, and the embarrassment...the act had already been committed; my baby was not the sin. I didn't really know anything about condemnation at that time, but I was condemning myself quite a bit and not even realizing it. The enemy was beating me up. The longer I thought about it, the more I kept telling myself, "I can't have a baby." I needed someone to talk to quick because I didn't want to tell my parents and I did not know what to do.

At the time, my Pastors were Harry and Lillie Reed. I went to talk to them. They opened their doors for me to come into their home, sat me down, and talked to me. I remember them telling me that the sin was in the act, the sex, not in the child. I really appreciated them ministering and counseling me. It was a very scary time for me, but at the same time, I was relieved that somebody else knew now. I knew it was time to tell my parents. As I sat at the kitchen table to reveal the news to my mom, I said, "Mom, I have something to tell you." She looked at me and she already knew. She was hoping that was not what I was getting ready to say, but it was. I cried. I could see the disappointment in her eyes as I sat there struggling to get it out. That was only one-step, the next step was telling my father. He didn't want to hear it from my mom; he wanted to hear it from me. I decided to come through their bedroom door with a plan whenever I got the nerve to tell him. I didn't tell him the same day, it was weeks, weeks later before I could build up enough strength and courage to tell him.

As I came to the room to release the news once again, I had my plan ready. Once I told him, he was disappointed, but wanted to know what I planned on doing. Well, I plan to finish my degree in business and then work for now. I had planned to get married, but I truly didn't even know where we stood at that time. It was like one of those 16 and pregnant things, but I wasn't 16, I was 18 and pregnant. A lot happened during that pregnancy that I talked about in 'T.O.O.L' (Trials, Tribulations, and Testimonies Out of Love). I have revealed this to give you a little backdrop if you haven't read my first book. I will now fast forward into the pregnancy. God had me covered the whole pregnancy and His eyes were on my unborn child and I. I knew God still loved me, but I knew He was not pleased with my decision.

The school I was attending was a little less than a two-year school, but I knew with the baby, I was going to miss some very important classes and possibly would have to make them up. Well, I worked my tail off getting ahead and trying to keep at least a "B" average in my classes. My man at the time came to see me at 31 weeks into my pregnancy. I was happy to see him, because I was going through this pregnancy without a partner. Well, we spent time together talking, reminiscing, and enjoying ourselves. The next day, I went to use the bathroom and I begin to bleed and clot. "Oh my Lord, I am bleeding." I didn't know what was happening, so I stored some of it in a Ziploc bag and headed to the emergency room. When they checked my cervix, I had dilated one centimeter. What? "We are going to have to keep you in here for observation to make sure you are not going into labor." The doctor said.

Next thing I know, here comes the nurse with a large needle containing steroids. This shot was going into my hip to help strengthen the baby's lungs in case of an early delivery. As I laid there not knowing if I was going into labor or what, I didn't have anything prepared. I had one more trimester to go, "No worries," is what I thought. Well, as they checked my cervix again, I had dilated another centimeter. The nurse said, "We are going to have to get you to a facility that can handle a premature baby." The hospital was 45 minutes to an hour away on a regular day, but it was in the middle of the December and snow was on the ground. "Oh, we will not be taking you by ambulance; you will be transported in a helicopter." "What?" I thought to myself. Did I mention I didn't have a bag or anything and I had to go to another city? "Really?" They wrapped me up, prepared me for the flight, and rolled me out to the helicopter. I was not sitting in the helicopter, they had me hanging from a strap from the ceiling, and it was cold. I couldn't see anything. All I knew was we were up in the air and then, we were flying. What a scary trip.

Finally, we made it to Stormount-Vail Hospital in Topeka, Kansas. They admitted me in the hospital and got me all hooked up to the meds. They were putting meds in my I.V. that would slow down contractions or going into labor early. I was thinking, "How long am I going to have to stay in here?" "You will be in here until we can make sure you will not have a preterm delivery," I was told.

"Okay." I said to myself. They would only allow me to have drinks and Jell-O at the time and I was hungry. As time progressed, the meds were doing their job and I had not contracted or dilated any more in a few days. I was now at 32 weeks and the next day was Christmas. The nurse and doctor told me since I was doing so well, I would most likely spend Christmas at home with my family. My family had been driving up to see me as much as they could. Yeah! I was excited. I was ready to get up out of the hospital and get back to life.

Well Christmas morning rolled in and the pain struck so bad. I was grabbing bed rails and in excruciating pain. As the nurses and doctors came in the room, they said, "you are in labor and you have dilated some more. We are going to give you some meds to relieve some of the pain and continue to try and stop the contractions." I remember laying there holding my dad's hand at one point and squeezing tight. As we all sat in the room, I begin to doze off to some soothing, slow gospel music. The room was quiet and everyone just waited and listened. Then, out of nowhere, the pain started up again and this time I could feel something getting ready to come out. "She's coming," I yelled. I can't hold it. The next thing I remember was seeing my dad fly out the door. The nurses told me not to push because the doctor was on his way. Don't push. I couldn't help it, by the time the doctor put his gloves on he was right on time as my baby dropped right into his hands.

Baby Kennedy was here. My Christmas miracle baby came at 32 weeks and 3 lbs. 3 oz.

She was so small and hairy. As I went to see her in the NICU (Neonatal Intensive Care Unit), I can't remember the name of the news station, but it was in Topeka, that came to the hospital to interview me since I was the first person in that hospital to have a baby on Christmas day. I'm looking a mess and a little drugged up and they are talking to me. Wow! I couldn't wait to see that air on the news. Baby Kennedy was finally here and I was happy and relieved to see my baby girl. Now it was time to give my little princess a first name. Since I love to write in cursive and the letters T, J, and H were some of my favorite letters, I decided on Tijah. My baby girl was no longer baby Kennedy but Tijah Kennedy. I knew I would have to leave her at the hospital after a couple of days and return home an hour away. I came to visit as much as I could while she was in the hospital. Watching her develop and grow, praying that she would soon be able to come home with me. They allowed me to call as much as I wanted to check on her progress. Although it gave me a little time to rest, I was ready for my baby to come home. I felt empty leaving without her, but I was ready to get out of the hospital.

"Where is daddy?" That was the number one question. Her biological father went back to Georgia a day before she was actually born. He came to see her once as a baby, then nothing. Here I am with a baby, not married, need daycare, milk, diapers and all the daily essentials to care for my baby girl. I lived with my parents at the time, but once my father bought that milk for the first time, I knew I was going to have to do something. I never thought I would be on WIC or any type of assistance, but pride was not about to get in the way of taking care of my child. God provided everything that I needed and showed us favor.

Just sitting back thinking about how God moved tremendously for Tijah and I is amazing. I had made up in my mind before she was one that I was going to begin giving my tithes no matter what. It may have seemed small to some, but when you are hurting for money and bills are still coming, it is big. I can tell you this; we never went without a meal, without clothes on our back or a roof over our head. God supplied everything. When I look back now, I think, "how in the world did we do all of that" and still make it? We made it because of Christ in our lives. I truly believe that if I did not belong to Him and trust Him, I would not be where I am now. I tell you through it all, I still had hope.

My dream of wanting more children was not over, but I just never knew that the journey I would face to see my dreams come to fruition

THE SECOND TIME
Chapter Three

"You may kiss your bride." "Yes!" I am married now in 2004 and I know babies are in our near future. A few months after being married to my wonderful husband, he received military orders to go to Ft. Wainwright, Alaska. "What?" This is going to feel like we are moving to Germany. We will be so far away from family and friends…then, in Alaska. I was in total shock. Getting to Alaska was no joke. When we got off the airplane it was 50 below zero, snow was everywhere, and my nose hair, eyebrows, and eyelashes began to freeze up. As soon as we hit the heated airport, whatever froze began to unfreeze. (Smile)

We were not in Alaska long before we began talking about a baby. In 2005, we decided that we would begin trying to conceive. Month after month yielded nothing. My cycle could run a few days late and I was running to the store to get a pregnancy test only for it to be negative time after time. My husband received orders again, but this time it was for the Iraqi war. He went the year before we married and they were sending him back. I was really looking forward to having a baby, but being pregnant with a little one at home already and him away at war; I guess God knew what was best. Time progressed and it was time for his R&R. He was returning home for two weeks and I knew we would try again. Waiting and anticipating and still nothing, why? "Why am I not getting pregnant?" My prayers for a baby between us became more intense, the desire got even stronger, and the disappointment of being patient was getting real. I don't know how many pregnancy tests I bought over the first few years, but it became addictive that needed to go.

As I was sleeping one morning, I could hear a small voice speak to me and say "Liberty." I was half sleeping, and heard it again, "Liberty." As I sat all the way up, I couldn't wait to tell my husband that God had given me the name of our baby and her name would be Liberty.

THE PUSH THE PULL AND THE PRAYER

Once I told him what I heard, no more than a week that passed by, and he had a dream. He told me about the dream. He said he was sitting on our bed holding a baby. They were gazing at one another recognizing she looked just like him but having my eyes. "Are you for real?" I said. Wow, it gave me a little boost in my spirit, because I believe God was listening to our hearts and desires. "She is beautiful." He said.

Almost two years had passed and I still was not pregnant, so I told my husband it had to be him, surely the problem wasn't with me. "Will you get checked out?" Because of the difference in our ages, I figured he was the problem. After the results came back, it showed he was fine. "What?" Oh, no, the realization that it must be me hit hard. I felt like Hannah. "How can I have one child and now not be able to have another?" "What is wrong with me?" "Why can't I conceive?" Surely, God is punishing me. When I went to the doctor, she told me to eat more green veggies and keep trying. "What, are you serious right now?" I was definitely not satisfied with that answer, there had to be more. Going home, I felt some kind of way. I had no other choice but to submit to the notion to keep trying.

From 2005 to 2010...every year, month, week, day, minute and second that passed, I had to PUSH (Pray Until Something Happens) I had to believe God will do it. Many nights of crying, and many days spent in disappointment, many years of trying, many people praying for us, laying hands on us; forth-telling we will one day have a child, but everything remained futile.

I was in my bedroom one day and I knew I had touched the hem of His garment and was made whole through prayer. I was in expectation of our miracle coming to life. I wrestled with God like Jacob. I said, "I will not let you go until you bless me Lord," but somewhere along the way it begin to get dim. Then we came across information on IVF (In vitro fertilization), a process by which an egg is fertilized by sperm outside the body. We begin to look into it. We prayed about it and went to check it out. If you know nothing about the process, it's no easy process. It is very time consuming, expensive, and many medicines must be taken before, during, and after the pregnancy. It was all the worth it because we wanted a baby.

First, I had to go see the doctor for consultation. Afterwards, I met with the doctor to get the results of the finding in my body. "LaToya, we have the outcome of the x-rays. They show the reason you are unable to conceive is because both fallopian tubes are blocked. They are damaged to the point that the eggs will not be able to pass through." "What does this all mean?' I thought. "So, are you saying I will not be able to get pregnant naturally?" The doctor told me that they could perform the IVF procedure and showed me their percentages for success. Still in disbelief, I asked, "Is there a way to open the tubes?" "Yes, you can choose that process, but there is no guarantee that you will get pregnant after you open your tubes, taking into consideration that they are not too damaged to be opened." "It's a six week recovery process and then another year of trying to get pregnant after the surgery."

"What?" We had already waited years and were not trying to wait any longer.

We gathered more information on the IVF procedure, the cost, time, etc. We were not sure this was the right path to take, but we were desperate for a baby. Then the shocking part of the process was released: "You will have to give yourself shots." "WHAT?" Shots in my stomach and hips in addition to the blood work that would take place each visit. I was a little nervous about all this, but I had to move forward. "I'm doing it." "We're doing it."

I never had so many appointments in my life, but it didn't matter, whatever it took. Let the process begin and begin, it did. Eggs were retrieved from me in order to add the sperm to the eggs and then insert them back inside later. The day was finally here to have the eggs placed back inside of me and wait for a few weeks to find out if it worked and I was with child. The wait seemed forever. Then the phone rang and it was confirmed. "Yes, you are pregnant." All kinds of feelings rushed through my head. I was crying, excited, and joyful to know that the process worked and I was with child. The shots, blood work, and appointments did not stop because I was pregnant. Returning to the office a few more times to look at our seed was amazing. She or he was so small and had not formed at the time. After a while, my appointments switched over to an OB/GYN and we were able to see the baby on the screen and then the sex. The baby was a boy! It was very exciting.

My husband was watching "I didn't know I was pregnant" on television one night after we found out the sex of the baby. There was a couple on there that went through a lot having their baby boy and he was more than a miracle. Their story was amazing and their son was amazing, and his name was Titus. We were like, "That's it, our son's name will be Titus! We went and read what Titus meant in the Bible. Titus was of Greek origin meaning "pleasing." Latin meaning, "saved." Titus was an early Christian converted and assisted Paul in his missionary work. This book in the Bible was a letter written on the subject of pastoral care in the early church. Titus was a "defender." The name had strong character.

Going back for a moment to ten weeks into my pregnancy, I had begun to bleed a little bit and had to make an appointment to see the doctor. I was told that it was not consistent bleeding and that some people may bleed sometimes during pregnancy. "Whew…okay." Shook me a little bit there. Then moving to the morning of December 31st. I was having some terrible pains in my abdomen; excruciating pain. I went into the Emergency Room and they admitted me in the delivery part of the hospital. They listened to the baby and then hooked me up for about an hour to a machine to see if I was having contractions. I was asked to give a sample of my urine to be examined as well. When the results came back, I was told that I had a urinary tract infection. They unhooked the equipment, gave me a prescription and I went home.

After taking the medicine, I lay down to sleep, but I still was not feeling better. I couldn't go to sleep and the pain was getting worse. I was thinking at this point, I do not want to miss watch night service because I wanted to give my testimony about the baby. The pain continued to worsen and I begin to draw my body together on the bed, groaning. Around 9:00 p.m. or so, I felt like I had to use the bathroom in between the pain, so I got up off of the bed to head to the bathroom.

I could feel a gush. Oh my God! Blood begin to fall on my carpet and trail me all the way to the bathroom. As I sat down to use the toilet, it continued to come out in large portions. I started crying and not knowing what to expect. The pain was still there and blood was flowing heavily. I thought it had stopped, so I got up and felt light headed as I went to the floor and blood was getting everywhere. Our bathroom was beginning to look like a real live murder scene. I cannot even explain how much blood was all over the bathroom…inside the toilet, on the toilet, on the carpet, and the floor… it was a mess. As I lay on the floor crying and feeling faint, my husband called 911.

911 arrived, put me on the stretcher, and carried me to the ambulance. They began to check my blood pressure and it was so high that they said I should have passed out. They asked me did I have a history of hypertension. "No." I have never had a problem with my blood pressure. My blood pressure usually ranges 111-120 over 80. This was very unusual. The ambulance rushed me to the emergency room of the hospital where they took me off the stretcher and admitted me in the delivery. As I lay in the bed continuing to bleed and still feeling the excruciating pain, they gave me an I.V. and then an ultrasound to check on Titus. Titus was standing up, breech, and it look like he was running. No exaggeration. I said, "He looks like he is running." Well, his little heart was beating slowly and I was losing a lot of blood, so they went to get blood for a transfusion. "What in the world was going on?" Blood transfusion. I never thought I would ever have to have that in my life, but I needed it. Between the I.V. and the meds, they were giving me, the pain began to lessen and I went to sleep.

Watch night service was over, we were in the New Year, and I was still pregnant.

Visitors came to see us on New Year's Day. Titus's heart rate was normal and my blood had lessened. We spent another night in the hospital for observation. During the midnight hours, I begin to feel pain again, so they had to add more meds to my I.V. to lessen the pain, but it continued to worsen. I couldn't turn to either side because it was hurting so bad, I could barely move. I remember the nurse I had that night was so mean. She was pushing my body this way and that way trying to do different things, whether it was to add a pad under my bottom again for the bleeding, or turn me to give me a shot. I was in so much pain and about ready to kick this woman. Her tone was nasty and her whole demeanor was mean. "I am laying here in all this pain, and you have an attitude today?" "Really?" As time progressed, it started to feel like I was going into labor. I felt something beginning to come out. I didn't want to push I was only 21 weeks pregnant, but he was coming. "Oh no!" "He is too early." "Why is this happening?" As the pain worsened, the next thing I knew he came out and there was complete silence. I saw the nurses run to the bathroom, and still silence. No cry, not a noise. "Where is my baby?" "What's wrong with my baby?" "Where is my baby?" Still nothing. I thought the worse, but I was still lying there hoping for the best. As the nurses came from the bathroom, they had Titus all wrapped up and left the room. I was told that my baby was a stillbirth. Filled with so much emotion and pain, I cried uncontrollably. "My son!" "Why?" "What happened?" "What went wrong?" I was a mess at that point. January 2, 2011, Titus Theodore Bilbo was born and went to be with the Lord.

Because of the hospital, Titus was born in addition to the fact he was over 20 weeks, they had to bury him instead of just getting rid of the body. "A funeral?" I happen to be over by one week and now a funeral. I couldn't believe what I was hearing. I didn't want to talk about a funeral, discharge or anything at this point; I just wanted to know why my baby could not be saved while I was in the hospital. "What happened?" They brought my baby to me wrapped in a blanket and cleaned up. Not a breath, there was no life. I held him tightly in my arms as I cried and said goodbye. I would have liked to see him grow up and be a little man, but God knew best. God must have known something that we did not know, so he was going home to be with Him instead.

I remember the next morning when it was time to be discharged, the woman that had been so mean had come back to wheel me out of the hospital in a wheelchair. Not a smile, not a word. She was so quiet and I could feel her uneasiness. I am sure she remembered how nasty she had been the night before and now she probably felt some remorse due to the current circumstances, but didn't know what to say. I was going home with no baby, going to my room with no baby, and going to bed at night with no baby. "God, why?" We fasted, we prayed, what happened? It was hard to sleep. It was hard to eat or think. I was so disappointed, hurt, and confused. Something we wanted so badly had just slipped through our fingers and suddenly there was nothing. No cry, no hand to hold, no diaper to change, no foot to rub, no cheeks to kiss, there was nothing. "How would I move on?" "How could we move on from this?"

Preparing the funeral, as the day drew nearer, it became more and more real. Going to pick out a casket, get programs made, and all the other things to prep became real. As the programs were being created, I was inspired to put a poem in there and this is what I wrote:

Titus, so small, so formed, so beautiful, and sweet.
We had only but a moment to see your full physique.
Your hands and feet so plain and complete.
Your face and nose looking like daddy and me.

As we held you in our arms, As you lay to rest,
All kind of thoughts racing through our minds,
Not understanding, but knowing that God knows best.

I miss each morning and each night,
That you moved around inside of me.
So busy you were, so strong you were,
Holding on until the very end.
We want you to know that the enemy did not win.

Although your time here was very short,
Your memory will last for a lifetime.
You are in a better place now,
A place where we all want to get to one day.

Your face, your touch, will forever be a part of us.
We miss you and we love you very much.

I remember sitting at the funeral as the poem was being read and the casket was sitting so close, just thinking of whom my baby could have been, what he could have done, and how I wish I could just hold him one more time. Then, they let the doves go in the air, which was symbolic of releasing but never forgetting our son Titus.

Days went by feeling like decades upon centuries. Many nights were spent crying and wishing it all could've worked out and somebody could have saved my son, but God...

This woke something up in me. It changed something in me, too. I was so busy in church at this point in my life until I had to take some time to just stop and pause for a moment. "Did I do this to myself?" I begin to think. All the running, going, meeting after meeting, event after event, project after project, allowing the enemy to inch in through an open crack of my life. This man of God should have never taken space in my life. It caused much confusion and interruptions. My thoughts were because it was ministry, the company would be good for growth and maturity. In retrospect, innocent conversations led to inappropriate conversations, which led to opening a door for Satan to sift me out. All attention is not good attention. Ladies and gentlemen no one is exempt. When your love language is words of affirmation believe me the enemy knows. A dead end, empty, unhealthy relationship is not the answer.

The pain just didn't seem to go anywhere. I was grateful for the encouragement and prayers that were coming my way, but the pain of losing my son was a hurt that I could not even explain. When you have been praying for something for so long, finally have it, and lose it all in one day. It hurt, but God. I remember telling someone that even though I may be sad, I know that my God knows best. I know that for whatever reason, God has my baby and he will turn these tears into joy. This sorrow will change. Anyone that has lost a baby, child, or had a stillbirth or miscarriage knows the pain that comes and sometimes there is no explanation.

I want to encourage someone today that God has a perfect plan for our lives, it may not be the plan that we want, but it's His plan. If we are seeking God and all of His righteousness, all these things shall be added onto us. All things will be taken care of in our lives. We must turn to God first for help, fill our thoughts with His desires, obey and serve Him in everything. We begin to put people, places, things, as priorities before God. Those categories of distractions begin to bump God out of the way. We become too busy with what we're involved in and we forget all about God and His plans for our lives. "What are our motives for our desires and dreams?" "Why do we want what we want?" "Is it for selfish gain?" "Is it for a greater good?" "Is it for ministry and helping others?" "Why do we want the things we want?" We have to sit back and reflect on the reason we do things. When we truly take the time to look at why, we may begin to see why not. "Why isn't it happening for us?"

We have to choose God first. God must be first in all we desire to do. He already has a plan from beginning to end, so why not go with what's already in blueprint and stop trying to change the picture.

- I encourage you today to seek God.
- I encourage you today to pray more.
- I encourage you to fast more.
- I encourage you today to check your motives.
- I encourage you today to love, give, be about more, focus, forgive
- Then watch how SUDDENLY God will move on your obedience.

THE NEXT ATTEMPT
Chapter Four

It takes time to heal from things that happen in life and we can't rush it.

About a year or so passed by and I began contemplating being pregnant again. I just knew that Titus was not the end. Even while I was pregnant with him, I knew there was more. I knew God had a child for us and she was coming soon.

We still had frozen eggs at the IVF (Invitro Fertilization) clinic and we felt we were ready to try again. First, we thought about the option of having my tubes opened up by the hospital, because Tri-care Insurance would pay for that. We had some eggs waiting, although we would have to go through part of the process again and pay quite a bit of money, as before. It was well worth it. We went back to the clinic so I could get some more drugs, shots, and prepare once again to have the eggs placed inside of me to see if they would produce a child. It was months of preparation and excitement. Just thinking about doing it again was overwhelming and exciting at the same time. I was not thrilled about taking shots and medicines again, however I was prepared and ready.

It was the week that we were getting ready for the transfer to happen and I begin to think of Titus again. Lord, I was missing him so much, but like Hannah I just knew God would give us a child. That would be like the Pastor told us a few months back, "double for our trouble."

I was in expectation for the baby we dreamed about and fantasizing about another child as well. My appointment was set for the following day. I took my morning meds, grabbed everything I needed to take to my appointment, and headed out for another transfer. We were about to do it the second time. I was a little bit anxious, nervous, and had inexplicable feelings at the same time. We had just parked and about to go inside the clinic when my phone was going off in my purse. Fumbling as women normally do racing to catch the caller before it stops ringing going to voice mail. Usually I put my phone on silent or vibrate, but not this time. "Let me see who is calling." I'm sure I had that bewildered expression on my face because it was the office to where we just parked to go inside.

"Hello, may I speak to Latoya Bilbo?" "Yes, this is she." I said. "Mrs. Bilbo, I really didn't want to call and let you know this, but your frozen embryos didn't make it." I was in a conundrum. "They didn't make it?" I said confused. "No ma'am, we retrieved the eggs to have them thawed out and they did not make it; we will not be able to transfer them." I remember looking at my husband and breaking down with uncontrollable tears like excruciating and torturing rips to my heart; just began to cry. "What do you mean they didn't make it, I'm right here." "I'm right here." This has to happen today. "I'm right at the door." "Ma'am, ma'am!" "This usually only happens to 1% of clients, it's very rare that the embryos will die like this." "Are you serious?" Oh, there was much contention and intentional anger to God. Despairingly, "Why?" "How could this happen like this?" It felt like another baby died. There was nothing further to do; because I had no eggs left at this point. The only thing we could do was to return home. What a ride home, upset and disappointed. I couldn't understand why it was not happening for us. "Why was God punishing me?" "Had I not been forgiven of past sins?" "Had I been cursed?" "Was there something generational going on?" "What was it?" I just didn't understand. God, I thought you promised me a child. I know I heard your voice God. I thought you promised us a baby. You gave me a name; you gave Bilbo a visual. I did not understand how I could wind up in the 1% of this happening. God must really have something special in store for us, but at this point, I could not open my eyes to see that. I was so hurt with disappointment.

As time went on, we begin to think about adoption. Maybe we are supposed to have our child through adoption. They always say it's hard to get a baby, but if God is in it, it will happen. We went to the adoption class that explained the process and how everything with DSS and other agencies worked. Wow! They said that it is true, most people desire to get a baby but it's very seldom what the agency had available. Instead, they had a lot of teenagers, children with disabilities, and other school age or toddler children. We had to do a little research, some more praying, and thinking. Our desire was a baby, but we will go ahead, fill out the information, and get this process started. Before and after the first meeting, we were both pseudo-excited about getting started. Weeks after the session, we begin filling out the paperwork, turning in assignments, and prepping to do other parts of the process when a few more weeks passed and all of a sudden, the desire just died. Simultaneously it seemed the death happened in both of us. We stop filling out paperwork; stopped talking about it; we just stopped. It was as if the desire died to go by way of adoption, DSS, etc.... I don't know what happened. Everything suddenly changed.

My husband and I begin taking more mini vacations and get-a-ways, enjoying our families and one another. I continued to ponder that God is able; I know God can, but if He chooses differently than our desires, we would yield to that. Just like the Hebrew boys, God delivered them, but the three had this resolve that if He didn't save them from the fiery furnace, they knew He was able and He could (capable and willing). I was not giving up on my dream to have a child with my husband! We were gaining a different perspective. We still held on to our desires, but didn't voice it as much anymore. It became internal between God and us. "God I know you showed my husband the baby and gave me a name, however you do it God however you do it. I trust you." We thought about our oldest daughter in high school who would be soon graduating. She may not want to stay with us while at college, but if she does; we will all spend some time on vacation and take time to enjoy one another as family. I never let go of the dream, but just chose to thank God for His timing.

So much was going on in my life. I could feel God moving tremendously in my house and things just were not the same anymore.

My eyes opened and life was changing. My surroundings began to change, which moves us into my next chapter.

IN PURSUIT OF ME
Chapter Five

I could feel God changing things inside me. I was uncomfortable with it and didn't know what to do. I could feel Him telling me "It's time." "It's time for what God?" As I was listening for an answer, He gave no response. I could sense in my spirit what He was referring to, but I didn't listen. Then, a second time I hear the word "Go." "Go where God?" However, nothing still. Then the third time I heard "Abraham shift." God was giving mandates, directive and at this point, I knew where this was going. I was not good with it because I wanted to remain in my comfortable and familiar place. I certainly didn't want to start over again. "Where will we go?" "What will we do?" It's crazy how so much pain, hurt and disappointment can have you captive in a place. The strongholds prevent you from leaving and make it almost impossible to pull away.

Considering my soul ties, strongholds, and comfort zones, how could I start new? God, I can't. We have done so much as a family here and we have sown so much. "Where shall our ability to reap go if we leave where we are right now, where we have been planting?" God was not saying a word.

Then, one day I was scrolling through my Facebook page and saw a post from Stephanie Kirkland and an "In Pursuit of Me" course that was happening in Columbia, SC and Charlotte, NC. Let me see what this is all about. As I begin to read the article, all I could see was "It's time," flashing in my face from the words in the article. It caused me to remember what the Lord had spoken earlier in the year. "It's time!" I knew this course was for me. I have to see how I can get more information, because it's time for something new. It's time for something new for me. If I didn't do something to help me, then I would be ineffective to help people I am supposed to reach in ministry.

After conversing with Mrs. Stephanie Kirkland, I knew this course was for me, so I signed up. The classes were not huge, so it made sharing, listening, and participating easier and more comfortable than if the group was too large where people could be lost or overlooked. As I went through this study on pursuing me, I rediscovered myself. I got tired traveling through dead end relationships, unhealthy soul ties, business, burn out, confusion, hurt and disappointment. God gave me instructions and mandates. Little did I know this course would push me into my new…the next chapter of my life. "Thank you, Jesus." We collaborated with one other woman in the class as an accountability partner. I love who God connected me with. From the first time we talked on the phone, it was like we had known each other for years. We clicked instantly. We had some things in common, we were able to be real with one another, and become transparent about some things.

Through the course, I understood whom my life is supposed to represent. Some people come in our lives at various seasons for what we can offer them, give them what they need and vice versa. When there is a lack in a person's life, that lack will attract them to you. Your name may be FAITH, VALUABLE, ORDER, HOPE, NEW, etc. My name is RESTORATION. As I dug deep into myself, every ugly part, every hurt part, everything that was a part of me, I could see where God had to rebuild and restore me. I needed to begin again.

I looked at a few relationships I developed and saw where they needed restoring. People saw their needs being fulfilled in me and that pulled us together. I also saw where I had to let some things go that I clamped on to for dear life. Being a military child, I felt I had to compensate for moving about constantly. I had to start building new everything each time we moved: new friends, new school, new jobs, etc. It was not easy at all, because when one comes into a new environment, cliques and bonds are already established. Therefore a newbies are not always welcome, but God connected me to whom I needed to be connected to in each season. I didn't realize it then, but in retrospect I see that is true.

In order for restoration to take place, I had to know the Restorer. He is always on ready, set, go! He wanted to restore me and make me better. Nevertheless, the responsibility was on me to renew my mind, my walk, my talk, and my attitude. He would do the rest; help me to rebuild relationships, order, protocol, vision, and purpose. The Lord with my permission would repair my broken places. Thank God for his carpentry skill. He had to renovate and recondition my thinking. God reestablished me. Not only did God do that, but He is still restoring things in my life through this process and journey. I pause in thanksgiving to Him.

Let me back up right quick. When I first drove over to see where the class would be held, it was astonishing to see it right across the street from the IVF office where I had gone for Titus and where my frozen embryos didn't make it. "My God!" I was like, "God really? Really? Right across the street, are you serious?" Each time I drove up to class I had to see the place where it didn't happen for me; the place where I lost what was promised by GOD! I was reminded of barrenness twice - I, LaToya was in the same company with Sarah and Hannah.

Going there was a disappointment, but hurt was not going to stop me from coming to the "assignment of time." Time passed as I thought about the three times God gave a mandate to me, "It's time." "Go." "Abraham Shift."

I was driving to work one morning and clear as day; the Spirit gave the fourth mandate, "If you do not leave, you will die." That thing hit me like a ton of bricks. "Lord, I know you are not playing games with me." I knew that God was serious and this was not the time to be selfish. This could affect my whole family and me. When God moves, it lines up. When God does it, there is no confusion, only peace. It was a struggle, but God. We were going to obey God, although we had no idea where we were going, we knew God had us. One day God will release me to tell the story of this journey, but right now is not the time. What I will tell you is that God can and will bring you out of dark, barren places, and give you life. You can choose to stay in a mess, or you can choose to listen to God's instructions and move in the things of the Kingdom. The enemy will try to make you believe that you have not heard God or that something is wrong with you. However, when you know that you know God's voice, that old enemy cannot trick you or deceive you any longer. "Amen!" God lined everything up. My God fearing husband and I were on one accord. He was already months ahead of me concerning what God was doing, but he wanted to give me time to be obedient and hear what God was saying to us as a family. I thank God for that.

He was not pressuring me, but allowing me to go through.

I think back to when a Prophet visited a ministry that I was a part of, I remember him telling me that God is mending your heart; your heart has been broken and God is mending it. I knew of some things that God was doing, but it wasn't until I faced this part of my journey and I was going through hurt and disappointments that I reflected back on what the man of God said, and that time was then. He was mending my heart. I was so broken in my spirit and my family, structure was falling apart, but I kept on being busy and smiling through it. "But, God!" The funny thing is I was dying and nobody knew it. I was operating, ushering, singing, worshipping, and praying but dying. How could there be so many people around, but nobody knew that spiritual death was knocking at my door? How could I be functioning but dying? This was a very hard place for me in my life. I was used to doing and doing and saying "no" was not easy for me to do. I would fill my plate with one task after another, not truly understanding that I was only one person. I was overeating in the ministry. I was literally glutting. I was a wife, mother, employee, woman of God who was stretching herself too thin. Burn out was sure to reach me eventually and that was the end result. It was nobody's fault but my own. My eyes had to be opened, and I thank God for sending a word, new life into my life.

I truly thank God for the sweet soul who was unaware of my struggle, but invited me to come to Bible study one night. She didn't know that we had left where we were, she just invited me out and I said, "Yes." I went to church on that Tuesday night and my God, Jesus must have told Pastor Turner all of my business. There was no Bible lesson that night; it was total worship, praise, prayer, and prophetic words coming forth. I couldn't even contain myself. As the words were being released in October 2013 in the ministry, I headed to the altar. I laid it all out there at the altar. I cried out to God, because I knew He knew, understood, and would restore me. I was ready for something new. I will never forget that night, because it changed my life.

While riding home, I continued to bask in the presence of God. He was still all over me and it felt amazing. I could barely wait to tell my husband about the service. "Babe, you have got to come with me to the next Sunday service." Sure enough the following Sunday, my family came. They enjoyed themselves as well. The praise and worship was on a different level. The Word was on point. There was something about the power of God that was moving in that place and I wanted more. I was hungry for more. As we continued to come, God was restoring me and life was returning to me. We learned what was in store for us. Somehow our facts were twisted. We learned that God is waiting on us, and not the other way around.

I just want to encourage someone today who may be facing a struggle where they have so much on their plate they cannot function the way they were created to function. It is okay to say NO. It is okay to say not this time. It is okay if you cannot do it all. You were not called to be on every board or ministry. We all have our gifts, abilities and talents and when we all operate and function in them together as a team, no one person will have to do it all. If this is not learned, you will reach burnout. You will begin to operate out of duty and not out of serving because you desire to please God. You will begin to operate out of guilt, manipulation or intimidation. Have you ever taken the time to ask yourself why you do certain things? Are you effective? Are you serving with pure intentions and with a pure heart? Are you pleasing God or man? It's time out for just piling up your calendar, agenda and plate with stuff. The more you add to it, the less effective each area becomes. Do you want to be more effective for Christ? Then focus on the areas that God has anointed and called you. I am not saying this to say that you cannot lend a hand where help may be needed, but you know your limitations. I encourage you to reexamine your whys.

Burn out will cause you to become disengaged and isolated. I can only tell you what I know from my own personal experience. We must maintain good health, sleeping habits as well as renewing our minds daily. If you are all a mess and neglected, then how can you truly help someone else? It's okay to take time for yourself and your family. If you haven't done this in a while, then stop waiting and take some time. We must be honest with ourselves and others as well. It is not always easy to be truthful when desire is not to hurt your brother or sisters feelings. In the end when you are not truthful about a situation, you wind up hurting yourself in the process. I'm not at all saying I have completely arrived in all these areas, but I am striving to be a better me. I want you to be a better you, so that you will operate just the way God created you to function. Amen!

GOD SUPERNATURALLY INTERVENED
Chapter Six

We were in church one Sunday morning and I remember hearing Pastor Turner say, "God is supernaturally intervening in your situation now." I felt that. I felt my spiritual baby leap. When we got home that afternoon, I told Mr. B, "I felt my spiritual baby leap today" when pastor said, "God is supernaturally intervening in your situation now."

"And it occurred that when Elizabeth heard Mary's greeting, the baby leaped in her womb, and Elizabeth was filled with and controlled by the Holy Spirit. In addition, she cried out with a loud cry, and then exclaimed, blessed (favored of God) above all other women are you! Moreover, blessed (favored of God) is the Fruit of your womb! (Luke 1:41-42 AMP) When we read this story an angel had first visited Mary and told her the Holy Spirit would come upon her and the power of the Highest will overshadow her, also the Holy One who is to be born will be called "The Son of God". The angel told her about Elizabeth who was with child in her old age and called barren. Now Mary is pregnant without knowing a man (having sex). *"For with God nothing will be impossible." (Luke 1:37 AMP)* As soon as Elizabeth heard Mary's voice, Elizabeth's baby leaped and she was filled with the Holy Spirit, which confirmed everything the angel had already spoken.

I say all that to say this, I truly believe that the Holy Spirit spoke those words through pastor's mouth and my womb lined up with my faith. My faith increased. God spoke and my spiritual baby leaped. First the spiritual and then the natural. God supernaturally intervened.

This happened sometime between January and February 2014. As February was passing by, I was a few days late on my cycle. I was unsure of what was going on, but this occurrence was nothing new. On the other hand, both my tubes were completely blocked, so maybe? No, I didn't put stock in that. Another week or so went by and I became concerned. Am I going through menopause? I wanted to believe I might be pregnant, but that was a hard sell based on the things that happened. I must be going through menopause. I tell Mr. B what's going on, and he tells me to go get a pregnancy test. "No babe, I really don't want to." He said it again, but I still didn't want to go get one. Later in the day, I decided, okay. I went ahead and got a pregnancy test and brought it home with me after work that night.

I came flying through the door like any normal day and ran upstairs to a place I rather dreaded, because I knew how addicted I had become to taking the test in the past. As I proceeded and waited for the results, I picked up the stick and did a double take. One line was negative, a cross was positive. It was a faded looking cross but it was still a cross. "Oh my God! Oh my God! Oh my God!" I yelled from the bathroom. Mr. B came running up the stairs to see what was going on. I showed him the stick and said, "It looks like I am pregnant. It's a little faded, but I hope that it's true." He told me to go get another one and do it again. I ran to the store that night and grabbed another box of tests. Back to the bathroom, I went to take the test again. As I proceeded and waited, the test was positive. I hollered again. "Oh my God! Oh my God! Oh my God!" That was still not enough. I had to make an appointment and go in and have the doctors draw blood to see if it was true. I had to wait until the next day and the anticipation was driving me crazy. I just knew that God had done exactly what He promised to do. I could just feel it.

It is now appointment time. My blood is drawn and they get a urine sample. It seemed like a marathon of waiting, waiting, and more waiting! The doctor returns to the room and says, "You are definitely pregnant." Then she says, "Should I be happy for you or sad?" I was like, "Happy! The doctors told me this could not happen because both my tubes were blocked, but God did it." " It's a miracle." She smiled and was excited too. "Yes, it's a miracle." The next step, it's time to find a good OB/GYN. Because of everything that had occurred, I wanted to see an at risk specialist, someone who would really take care of us after all that we had gone through in the past. That's exactly what we got. I knew I was pregnant but it was still so surreal. God did it. God answered our prayers. God didn't forget about me. "Wow!" I was an emotional wreck with excitement. I wanted to tell the world right away because it was a testimony that only He could get the credit for. We decided to wait because it was still so early in the pregnancy. It was like holding water in a container that is about to burst. I couldn't hold it any longer. We have to tell it. We have to tell it. So we decided on whom to tell, just so we could share the goodness of the Lord, especially to those that knew our story.

Our families were so excited and happy for us. God did it. I still had to tell a few of my friends, but I wanted to do it without saying it out of my mouth. I came up with the flyer that had a prenatal vitamin bottle on it and beside the bottle was a nice little paragraph, but the headline read, "Guess who's expecting?" As I watched them read it, their reactions were so memorable and heartwarming. I cannot forget about three reactions. Out of those three women, I don't know which one was the funniest. You remember what you did? I will call you out and then you think back. Helen, Renee, and Cynthia. "Wow!" You all made my day with those reactions. Somebody almost made me crash, woke up the neighborhood, scared the church folk and cried, and last; someone couldn't get any words out and just cried like a baby. "I love it!"

I really begin to think about "Liberty" now. We had been praying for her by name and Mr. B had seen her in a dream so, I just knew this had to be her. We set up appointments to do my monthly examinations and more because I was about to be 35 soon. They like to do extensive genetic testing to make sure that the baby does not have Downs-Syndrome or any other birth defects. Not only would the results be able to look at the chromosomes and tell us about defects, they would also be able to tell us the gender of the baby. Here we were, yet again waiting in anticipation to know. If you thought I wanted to wait until delivery, you thought wrong. No ma'am, no sir, I was ready. Then, the call came and the nurse was telling me all about the tests and that everything turned out well, etc....and that was all. I was thinking, "Hello, what's the gender of my baby?" She asked if I had any questions. Well, of course I did! "Do you know the gender of my baby?" I could hear her chuckle a little bit. "You want to know?" "Um, Yes." She proceeded to tell me, "Your baby is a girl." "YES!"

"Thank you."

I couldn't wait to call Mr. B and tell him, "Liberty is here, Liberty is here!" This was only the beginning. There were so many appointments and ultrasounds ahead of us. Not to mention the medications to help ensure that Liberty stayed in the womb as long as possible. I found out that one of the shots I had to take was 17OHP (Progesterone shots), and cost over $1000 per shot. I needed to have the shot once a week. "How in the world are we going to pay for this?" After talking with our insurance company about the outcome of my previous pregnancies, God showed me favor and every shot was covered. "Hallelujah!" Although I had to have the doctor's office give the shot every week, it was all a part of the process. The team was very knowledgeable and kept us informed of everything that was going on with the baby and me. Baby Liberty was growing just like she needed to be. All was going well. I think we were both still trying to wrap our minds around the fact that we were actually going to have a baby and man didn't do anything, it was all God. "Wow!" God had supernaturally unblocked my tubes. He had supernaturally intervened in our situation and a miracle was manifested in my womb. "Hallelujah!"

THE PROCESS
Chapter Seven

Time for another ultrasound and what did they see? Placenta Previa. My placenta was not in the right position...it was laying lower than it should be. The Web Dictionary says, "Placenta Previa is an obstetric complication in which the placenta is inserted partially or wholly in the lower uterine segment. It is a leading cause of vaginal bleeding. It affects approximately 0.4-0.5% of all labors." They told me not to be too concerned about it at the time because the Placenta could slowly change positions as I went further along in my pregnancy, so they would watch it with the numerous ultrasounds.

On a visit for another ultrasound, they noticed something else...a vein out of place, known as Vasa Previa. "What in the world is that?" We had never looked up the terms before, so we were curious about what they both were. Vasa Previa - is an obstetric complication in which fetal blood vessels cross or run in close proximity to the external orifice of the uterus. These vessels are at risk of rupture when the supporting membranes rupture, as they are unsupported by the umbilical cord or placental tissue. "WHAT? Explain that again?" I thought to myself. I had a vein across my cervix area and if my placenta erupted like before with Titus, or if I had a vaginal birth it could kill the baby and I. This condition is very rare, occurring in only one out of every 2,000 pregnancies. They seemed pretty calm for this to be this serious.

"How serious is this?" Well, they would have to keep a watch on it and they did not want me to go into labor when the time came around. What they suggested was performing a C-section at 35 weeks of pregnancy. "A C-section, oh, no!" I didn't want to be cut on, but whatever it took to get Liberty here safely was all that mattered at this point. Not only did they see the Vasa Previa but also they told me they also saw a nice size fibroid. "What the world?"

The fibroid was not causing harm to anything and it wasn't bothering me, so it was not a concern at the time.

After the appointment, I had to go home and research Vasa Previa and Placenta Previa. "Why in the world did I do that?" I wanted to be well informed of side effects and what might happen. I could feel myself begin to get a little scared, but I had to encourage myself. Just thinking I have two things going on right now that are not very common and that can be fatal. "God, I know you did not cause Liberty to come forth and then something happen to take her. She shall live and not die. I shall live and not die." Then I begin to thank the Lord for both of our lives. I knew God would get the glory out of this pregnancy, this testimony, and that I would tell the world. "Man didn't do it, but God did." That calmed my nerves and spirit and I was able to carry on.

The weeks and months seemed long because I was becoming a little anxious to see my princess, but I had to wait. I didn't want her coming too early. Wednesday, September 3, 2014 came. On this day as I was walking out of the building to go on break to my car, I came to some cement steps and completely lost my balance and slid across the ground and fell on my stomach. "Oh my gosh!" I just laid there for a moment in disbelief that I just fell on my baby. As I begin to pick myself up, my arms were scratched and bruised, my knees were bleeding, and the thought of what my baby just had to endure would not leave my mind. I was becoming more afraid as the seconds rolled by. I went back into the building to tend to my outer wounds and clean them up and told my supervisor I had to go to the doctor right away. Not wasting any time, I called my doctor and they told me to go to Labor and Delivery in the hospital. I did just that. Driving myself to the doctor I was trying to get my mind right, but I had just fell on my stomach. Mr. B met me there and we stayed there the rest of the day while they monitored movement of the baby and the baby's heartbeat and to see if there was any internal bleeding. By 4:00 p.m., all was well and they were able to release me, but they wanted me to get some rest and gave me a note to be off from work a few days. "Thank you Jesus!" I didn't know it then, but my time after the fall was about to get worse. A few days went by and I was fine, then I started to bleed. "Oh no, not this!" I called the doctor and was immediately told to go back to Labor and Delivery. Because I had Vasa Previa, no one was supposed to be poking and prodding anywhere near my vagina. The wrong move and the vein could burst. Back on the monitors again for hours and of course, each time I could not eat anything the whole time I was there. I was not really thinking about that until everything was looking okay, then my stomach would sound off. I could not eat just in case they had to do emergency surgery. When the doctors were aware of my condition, they wanted to observe me for a couple of days, so I had to stay in the hospital.

Shots, test, blood work, needles, nurses, machines, I.V.s, and monitors…. I was so ready to go after about two days, but they wanted to make sure that everything was all right before I left. I remember them moving me to another room because I did not have to be monitored as much, and this room meant going home was a high possibility. The doctors came around for the morning shift and I was told, "You can go home but you will be on bed rest. You will not be able to return to work, and you need to limit all activities at home and no sex." Well, we had already been told a while back about the sex part because of the vein, so that was nothing new. I was released from the hospital Thursday, Friday returned to my job to let them know what was going on, and to get my worker's compensation stuff I had to tell them that I would be on bed rest. "What will I do at home until Liberty was ready to come?" I knew I must finish my book, so I can get it published before the beginning of the year. I was about to get some stuff done, whatever project I could work on in bed. Friday at about 11:45 p.m. or so, I woke up and felt like I had to use bathroom, and then I felt a gush. From the bed I ran to the bathroom while blood begins to pour out from me. Oh No! It would not stop coming….more and more blood all over the toilet and the floor. My mind went back to Titus as I looked across our room at the bassinet. No, not again. I begin to cry aloud. I couldn't believe the same scene from December 2010 was happening again. I begin to cry out "We shall live and not die" "We shall live and not die" "Liberty shall live, Liberty shall come forth." "Devil you are a liar. I don't care what it looks like." Mr. B hurries and calls 911 and tells them what is going on. They tell me to get a towel or a blanket and lay down on my side, on the floor. I could hardly get to the floor with all the blood coming. I couldn't feel my baby move anymore. "Lord, help me."

As I got down on the floor, the bleeding did not stop and the towels and blankets were filled. I was crying and holding my stomach, but believing God for the best.

The emergency responders came in to get me up off the floor, carry me downstairs, and roll me out to the ambulance. I am sure this scene was all too familiar to the neighbors that remember it happening years back. We sat in the ambulance, which seemed like an eternity just to get an I.V. started. My blood pressure was good. Remember, last time it sky rocketed. I was not cramping. I still had not felt my baby move, but I was not in any pain. The bleeding had slowed down as well. As we begin to pull off, they asked me if I wanted to go to the nearest hospital. "NO! I went there last time and I cannot return there, take me to where I have been going downtown and they will be able to help me there." We set off for Palmetto Richland. They were still trying to poke me to get a good vein for the I.V. My veins are hard to work with at times and this just happens to be one of those days. Mr. B was back at the house trying to clean up the mess before heading out to the hospital. Well guess what, by the time we got to the hospital and they rolled me up to Labor and Delivery, my better half was standing up there highly upset. "How did he make it there before us? Where in the world were we? What is going on?" This was not funny then, but when we both look back now, he said as they had me reeled up so high on the ambulance bed rolling me in, sitting up, my face was completely calm and even a gentle smile on my face. I rolled in like there were no worries in the midst of the turmoil. I know that was nothing but God, because from the scene at the house to reaching the hospital, I felt as though God had touched me. Liberty had not moved, but I just felt that she was okay.

They got me into a room and we waited. I was monitored to see if dilation started, and if the blood was still coming. As they hooked up the monitor for the baby on my stomach, they found a heartbeat. "YES!"

Liberty was still alive and her heartbeat was great. Finally, she moved when she felt that machine come back on her. "Thank you Jesus!" It wasn't over yet, with all the bleeding I still had to be monitored and since this was my third visit to the hospital, when the doctors came to see me they told me I would be staying until I delivered. "WHAT THE WORLD?" They told me we are still looking at 35 weeks until delivery and we will be doing a C-section. I was happy Liberty was doing well and the bleeding had stopped, but now I had a long road ahead of me. I know God used this time to do some personal things within me and to enable me to see some things as well. It was a process and I was about to do some growing as my baby continued to grow. "My God!"

Lying in the bed all hooked up to the I.V. machines and monitors was no joke. I was uncomfortable, but I knew it was best because they were monitoring Liberty and making sure both of us were okay. From sun up to sun down, I waited each day for the doctors to make their rounds and give me new information or updates. From the blood work, they were able to tell that the bleeding did not cause Liberty any stress and she was doing very well. Her movement had certainly increased because the nurses could barely keep her heartbeat on the monitor. She was over here, over there, breech, head downward, and sideways. Little mama was changing positions and really busy. Each day was going well and better than the day before. I remember one day I was thinking they might just send me home since I was doing so well, so I did my little make up and was preparing for some good news. They laughed at me and said, "Mrs. Bilbo, you will be with us for a while." "Aww, man!" These were some long days and long nights, having to get assistance to shower and carrying cords and machines to go use the bathroom. God, I thank you that I don't have to live like this every day. I thank God for the ones that took time out of their busy day to day schedule to stop by and check on me. I thank God for those who brought me things to do and to pray. I even had an angel come and have morning devotion with me. That was great! I wanted to name names but I didn't want to forget anyone, so I decided I better not. You know who you are and I appreciate you and the love that you showed my family and me by being present. My husband was awesome, too. Running around trying to go to work, check on me, sit with me, and take care of Tijah and our home. He prepared our home for Liberty's arrival as well as making changes for us, too. Tijah came and stayed during the weekend. My sister came and stayed one weekend, as well.

This helped some of the time go by, but as the month grew into my second and ½ week, it seemed like the walls were closing in on me. Looking at the same menu day after day choosing breakfast, lunch and dinner, watching the same shows on Television, falling asleep from tiredness and hardly being able to stay focused on reading, twisting and turning, waiting in anticipation of them letting me go home.

September 22nd & 23rd brought a larger episode of bleeding. There were smaller ones leading up to these dates, and I was told the next time I have an episode they were going to do surgery. Where here I was with another episode that caused me to lose a lot of blood and pass a clot about as huge as a baseball. I thought a head was coming out. I had begun to have contractions and then the bleeding started. The nurses were coming to check my cervix again, they did not want my water to break or for me to go into labor. As they were checking my cervix, that's when the clot passed and the pain rather went away. I knew for sure they were not going to let me go home now. I was going to be in this hospital until I had my baby. At this point, I could not eat or drink anything, just in case they were going to have to take me in for surgery.

On the 23rd, my mother-in-law and three sisters-in-law came to the hospital to see us. I truly thought I was going to be having the baby that day because of the blood, but they wanted to continue to wait. They checked my blood levels again and I needed to have a blood transfusion. "No, not this again." This brought back memories of Titus once again. Now one arm was hooked up to one I.V. and the other arm hooked up to the blood transfusion I.V. My stomach hooked up to the monitors. I tried my best to keep a smile on my face in the midst of all that was going on. As the doctors came to visit, one of them did mention that every time they came in the room to see me I had a smile on my face. If only they knew what I felt inside, but God.

Early in the morning of September 24, I woke up and I heard the Lord say, "You and Liberty are covered in my blood." "Hallelujah!" Hearing those words, gave me comfort, encouragement and a revival in my soul.

me and gave me power. I knew that God had us covered and nothing was going to harm us. Although it looked bad at times, I knew that no weapon formed against us was going to prosper. We will live and not die. I was able to go back to sleep in peace. "Thank you Jesus."

Although I was bleeding uncontrollably at times, the doctors could not explain why it was not affecting Liberty. Her heartbeat was stable; my blood pressure continued to be good and my blood levels were stable until I needed the two blood transfusions from the last incident. I knew God was in control in the midst of it all, that's why I could still smile.

As I lay in the bed and the nurses came around to do some vitals and checks on me, one nurse said "You are basically a sitting time bomb" "What in the world?" "The devil is a liar." I thought that was a very negative comment although they may have seen that as a fact because of the various things I had going on inside my body. Keep that negative talk to yourself, all I need right now is life and positive words. Looking at all the blood loss, Placenta Previa, Vasa Previa and past history of my other pregnancies I was a special case that they wanted to keep a close eye on 24/7.

Week 31 of pregnancy and they are still trying to wait until week 35 to do a C-section.

The longer Liberty can stay in the womb the better. By the weekend of week 31, I was at a point of breakdown. I was tired of being in the hospital, looking inside the same four walls, and when the visits slowed down, I just had a breakdown. I don't know what came over me this day but I had had enough of the needles, the medications, the I.V.s, monitors, the bed rest. I just wanted to tell them to go ahead and do the C-section. Are we just going to keep waiting until my placenta abrupt or my vein pop? What are we waiting on? I keep bleeding and each time, you say the next time. I was really in my feelings at this point.

I remember talking to my father and they wanted to come and visit but were unsure when Liberty might get here, because they were heading somewhere for vacation. Then I remember him saying, "she is going to come on Thursday, October 2nd." I was like, "maybe she will come today," I think it was the end of September. He said, "She coming on the 2nd, watch." Well I rolled into week 32 and Liberty was still being Liberty active as she could be. Then it was Thursday, Oct 2, no bleeding, all was well. The hubby and I were just chilling in the room and Kimberly came to visit on this day. We sat for a couple of hours talking, catching up and cracking up. Then, all of sudden I felt a gush. I looked and I had started to bleed again. I called and the nurses' team came running in. As they checked out how much blood, it was and my cervix, they said they would get with the doctor and get back with me. When they came back to the room, they said it was not enough blood. I was sitting there looking at the blood like, "it's not enough?" Are you serious? However, when the doctor on call for that night came and seen how much it was, he said, 30 minutes and you will be going into surgery. "What the world?" 30 minutes, there was barely time to call, text, or do anything, because they had to prep me, clean out this room and move stuff to another room for after delivery. My dad had spoken that up and I guess Kimberly sealed it. Smile. I was being rushed into the surgery room for a C-section. I had been ready, but now I was getting a little worried, because I never had a C-section before and there were over 10 people in the room. The room was full of bright lights, tools, equipment and me. They begin to prep my back for the spinal tap. I couldn't get the epidural because it was too close to receiving emergency surgery and I couldn't wait that amount of time for the epidural. Leaning forward waiting for them to stick a needle in my back was a little nerve wrecking, but I had no other choice. Finally, it was time. "Lean forward and don't move," she said. All of a sudden I could feel this pinch in my back and it was in. Not too long after I felt the insertion, I could feel my body beginning to go numb. Wow, this was weird. Then I received some more meds as they stretched my arms out to the side. I thought about Jesus on the cross with His arm stretched wide. "God, I know you are with me." After checking to make sure I could not feel anything, they began the surgery.

Not too long after it started, I heard a loud cry. "Oh my God, Liberty!" I could hear her loud cries one behind the other. My baby! Mr. B went off from by my side to go take pictures of her and to cut the cord. A few minutes later, they brought her around to me so I could see her. So beautiful! She was so beautiful, light and small. That's my baby girl. Then they took her to go get hooked up in the NICU (Neonatal Intensive Care Unit) where she would be until she was able to keep her body heat, gain some more weight, suck, swallow and keep her milk down, and also be able to at least drink one to two ounces per feeding. This was already so familiar to me from my first child, Tijah who also stayed in the NICU for about three weeks.

Heading into the recovery room, the pain was terrible. They didn't want to waste any time so they wanted me to get up, shower, and use the bathroom, I had to have three days with no complications before it was time for me to go home. Here I was once again, about to go home and leave my baby at the hospital. Whether I was lying down or getting up, I was in pain. I had to have more shots, more medicines, and then they wanted to give me another blood transfusion because of the loss of blood during the surgery. I did not want any more I.V.'s or transfusions. I could regain my blood levels but it would take time, but in the meantime, I might be weak. At that point, I didn't care. I will just be a bit weak until I regain my blood levels, because I'd had enough. Time progressed and I finally felt like riding the wheel chair to go see Liberty. My husband had already been numerous times the day of, and the next day to see her and take plenty of pictures for me. Now it was finally my turn to see my little princess.

I was sitting there, looking in the incubator and there she was God's miracle. God's word manifested was breathing and alive. None of the pain, none of the time spent in the hospital mattered at this point because God did it! The emotions and gratefulness that ran through my veins were shouting for joy and victory. God had done what man said was impossible. A long road ahead for little mama in the NICU, but I knew God was in control.

It was around the third day or so of Liberty being in the NICU hooked up to all the cords and machines that she pulled the stuff right out of her nose. She was removing stuff and being very active. This was no surprise to me, knowing how busy she was in the womb. She was smiling and even opening her eyes a bit. Holding her in my arms and looking down into her face, I was able to tell God thank you again. Nine years and she was here. "Thank you Jesus!" It brought joy to my heart and tears to my eyes to see what the Lord had done. God remembered us...God remembered me.

ABRAHAM AND SARAH...
Chapter Eight

Wow! My mom called me one day while I was in the hospital and we got to talking about Abraham and Sarah and by the time we were finished talking, I saw us in them. *"1 Now Sarai, Abram's wife, had borne him no children. In addition, she had an Egyptian maidservant whose name was Hagar. 2 So Sarai said to Abram, "See now, the LORD has restrained me from bearing children. Please, go in to my maid; perhaps I shall obtain children by her." And Abram heeded the voice of Sarai. 3 Then Sarai, Abram's wife, took Hagar her maid, the Egyptian, and gave her to her husband Abram to be his wife, after Abram had dwelt ten years in the land of Canaan. 4 So he went in to Hagar, and she conceived. And when she saw that she had conceived, her mistress became despised in her eyes."* Genesis 16:1-4

Sarai, at the time had a back-up plan. God had already promised them a son, but because the situation didn't look favorable, they figured they would help God out. "God, you are not moving fast enough. God I want it now." God must be expecting it to come this way or that way. We get ahead of God and work out our own plans, when God already has a set time for everything. "But My covenant I will establish with Isaac, whom Sarah shall bear to you at this SET TIME next year." Genesis 17:21. We have to make the choice to wait on God.

Their story made me think of us. We had been trying to conceive since 2005 and all the months of trying and trying and nothing happening became very discouraging. Then, to have a baby name, for my husband to have a visual of her, and still nothing happening was really hard. We waited another year, and another, and still no baby. "Were we supposed to adopt?" "Was somebody just going to drop a baby off at our doorstep?" "How was this going to happen?" "God I know you promised me that I would have a child." Once I heard her name clearly and then my husband saw himself holding her, it was only a matter of time, still nothing. We both scheduled appointments to be examined and the problem was my fallopian tubes. Both of my tubes were completely blocked and there was no way anything was getting through those damaged tubes. Really? I guess God was not going to do it naturally, so we looked for other ways of becoming pregnant. We went to informational meetings for IVF and we prayed about it. I guess we wanted it so bad, we heard it was okay to proceed. I felt that God would do it by means of the IVF procedure. We had a Hagar plan. When that plan failed twice, we begin to look at adopting. Don't get me wrong, I believed that God was going to bring us our promise child; I just didn't know how he was going to do it. Adoption was exciting at first, but then we both just lost interest at the same time. It was so weird, but it was like something hit us and if God was going to do it, He was going to do it through me, His own way.

I focused my prayers on a supernatural healing in my body…a supernatural breakthrough in my tubes. I said like the three Hebrew boys, "God even if you don't do this, I know you can and you are able to do it, but while I wait, I am going to praise you. While I wait God I am still going to worship you like she is already here." Not every day was an easy day, but I was not going to give up on what I believed I heard God say was mine.

No matter how crazy it might have sounded, I was going to proclaim being pregnant and speak continually of having a baby, regardless to what it looked like.

When you think about Abraham and Sarah, they were old in age. At a certain age, we know things will not operate as they were operating before. Sarah's menstrual cycle most likely had gone away, she had passed the childbearing age in man's eyes, but God! God took a barren womb, a womb that should have been dead, a womb that was old, a womb that had passed childbearing age, and he performed a miracle! His word did not return back void. Abraham and Sarah had their promise child, Isaac.

When the doctors looked at my situation and saw that both my tubes were blocked and damaged, there was no logical way I was going to get pregnant without man's help, but God! God took an impossible situation and made it possible. God took our words, our prayers, our faith, our hearts and His words and manifested our miracle. God's promises are yes and amen. Hallelujah! It may have taken nine years, but it was for a greater reason than we know. God's plans and ways are higher than ours. He will step in and do the unexpected in His timing. He operates in eternity, not in our timing.

I just want to encourage someone reading this book today that you may have been waiting one year, a few years or even a decade to see something manifest and it still has not happened. Don't give up on God, for whatever reason God has you waiting; it's for a greater purpose. God's timing is never our timing, but he is never late. Amen!

WOUNDS AND SCARS ARE NOT A WASTE
Chapter Nine

When I think back to my last two pregnancies, the one attempt, all the shots, blood drawn, needles, medicine, and all the appointments, I realize that some folk might not have made it through such chaotic conditions. The enduring grace of God thrusted me forward and I survived. His grace is sufficient for my situations. I am aware there are people who have to give themselves shots every day due to diabetes and other illnesses. However, having this kind of power or responsibility at the end of a needle for a nervous and desperate mother, giving herself shots daily to help with the process of getting pregnant was some kind of task. Then while pregnant the grueling process seemed endless. Day after day got old, but when I considered about the results, I refuse to consider my own body, and focus on the promise, and the prize, then my God, the blessing kept me pressing!

When I look at my hands and wrists, I can still see where the I.V. needles had been inserted. It makes me think about how Jesus had nails pierced through his hands and feet, and how much He loves us that He bore all the pain. My God! Jesus bore it all for you and me. *'But he was wounded for our transgressions, he was bruised for our iniquities: the chastisement of our peace was upon him; and with his stripes we are healed."* (Isaiah 53:5) He was beaten past recognition and paid the ultimate price for our lives, and we are not a waste. Thank you Jesus. I can still feel from the C Section where my stomach in areas is numb, but God! I look at my hands and then I look at my baby and say, "Thank you, Jesus." My situation was not a waste, it saved my baby's life!

Man and woman of God, be encouraged today. You may have scars and wounds from things that have happened to you in life. You may not understand the "whys" or there may other unanswered questions you need answered. There is something about the power of God that can heal every scar you have from the inside out. When we look at the visible scars on our body, it's a daily reminder of what happened during that season or situation in life. In January 2013, I wrote a devotional on SCARS and I will share it with you here:

S. Something
C. Continuously
A. Activating
R. Rooted
S. Situations

Do YOU have any SCARS?

S.C.A.R.S are deeper than what is on the surface. We can see visible scars on our exteriors and identify them. There are SCARS that are invisible from our hearts and soul, it is harder to pinpoint because we use pleasure or pain to cover it up like band-aid to an open wound. You could use an antiseptic, but if the wound is not properly treated, infection will set in and cause a deeper problem.

The SCAR causes you to cry all over again, as if a thing has just happened. this SCAR causes you to feel the emotions that you felt way back when; this SCAR causes you to feel less than, unworthy, useless, disgusting, filthy, a mess, stressed and not only think negative, but it effects your talk, your walk, your communication, your health, it affects you."

SCARS cannot just be polished, wiped off, bandaged up, and expected never to resurface. We need a TOUCH from God to heal us from the inside out. We are healed from the inside, beneath the surface, those SCARS that used to activate, no longer have power; no longer have access; no longer have control; no longer can dominate who we are as people of God. When we earnestly seek God to heal us everywhere we hurt, not just some places, not just the places that you think people can see, but the deep places that nobody knows about. God is ready, man and woman of God, to take those SCARS and heal them from beneath the surface.

When we look at the physical side of scars, they are marks created during the healing of damage to the skin or tissues. A scar is a manifestation of the skin's healing process. After skin or tissue is broken, the body releases collagen to mend the damage. Collagen, a protein, reattaches the damaged skin. As the wound heals, a temporary crust forms and covers it. The crust is a scab that protects the damaged area.

Now, what exactly am I trying to get across? A SCAR is result of the healing process, but in the spiritual, if what is in us is rooted and we are still hanging onto pass hang-ups, setbacks, failures and disappointments, and have not let them go, that scab that protects the scar can be opened again. To God be the glory, that with God's covering, when God heals us from the inside out, His blood covers the SCARS, and by His power, we are healed, we are delivered, we are free in the Name of Jesus! Amen!

I say to you on this day that although the scars you have may have come from a hard, dark, or even barren place, it is not a waste. Nothing you go through or face is a waste. *Although man may have meant it for evil, God will turn it around for your good!* Believe that because it is in the word. *(Genesis 50:20)* You will come to a point in your life where you will look at your scars and rejoice because you know what God has brought you out of and through. Hallelujah! Thank you Jesus! You will look at how God has healed you, delivered you and set you free; how you are no longer in bondage because of what happened to you. Thank you, Jesus for freedom on today.

The wounds and scars that you have are not a waste. I can look at my hands now, and thank God. I can look at my stomach now, and thank God. I can look at myself now, and thank God. God is great and even surpasses that. Amen!

BLOOD TRANSFUSION
Chapter Ten

Now, this is not to insult anyone's intelligence, but I like defining words I reference. That way we all have a better understanding and be on the same page.

A blood transfusion is a safe, common procedure in which blood gave to you through an intravenous (I.V.) line in one of your blood vessels. Blood transfusions replace blood lost during surgery or due to a serious injury. A transfusion is given if the body can't make blood properly because of an illness. During a blood transfusion, inserted is a small needle to an I.V. line into one of your blood vessels. Through this line, you receive healthy blood. The procedure usually takes one to four hours, depending on how much blood you need. Blood transfusions are very common. Each year, almost five million Americans need a blood transfusion. Most blood transfusions go well. Mild complications can occur. Very rarely, serious problems develop.

When I think back to the bathroom scenes at my house during the pregnancy with Titus and Liberty, it was a mess. I lost so much blood both times. I never thought that I would need a blood transfusion in my life, but things happen in life where the unexpected might just pop up at your doorstep. I had to get two blood transfusions with Titus, and two more while I was still pregnant with Liberty. They wanted to do another one after my surgery, but I refused to have any more, I would just let it come back on its own, slowly but surely.

When I laid back and thought about the various blood transfusions that I have had, I could not help but look at it spiritually. "Whose blood do we have running through our veins?" It was a joke made a while back that I didn't know whose blood was running through my veins.

Naturally, I didn't know, but I began to look at it spiritually. I have "new blood" running through my veins that was given to me by my Father. I am going to take the natural definition from up top and give you my version of it, and it goes something like this:

A blood transfusion is a safe transfer of blood from Jesus's body into your body by faith and belief in who He is. A transfusion cannot take place if you do not first believe He is real. When you have faith that He is real and you accept Him into your heart, the transfusion begins. Your old blood has to be replaced with new blood. Although there may not be a natural needle you see, you can look at the cost Jesus paid on the cross for your sins and that cross is where the transfusion takes place for you. A natural transfusion may take one to four hours depending on how much blood you need, but a spiritual blood transfusion takes place suddenly. As soon as you accept Christ into your life, you have new blood running through your veins. Now, this blood never loses its power, but you may fall or fail in life and need the blood to cleanse you over and over again during your lifetime. The transfusion is not just a "once a year" thing. You need God's blood every day of your life. Without His blood, you are powerless against the devices of the enemy. You are powerful through Him and Him alone. When His blood is activated inside of you, death may be knocking at your door, but life is coming out of your mouth. The blood heals, delivers, and sets you free. Hallelujah! You change and stir up the atmosphere because of your daddy's blood on the inside of you. "My God! Do you know what's running through your veins? It has power!" Check your bloodline.

THE PIT, THE PRISON AND THE PALACE
Chapter Eleven

When I think about Joseph thrown in the pit, and then the prison from false accusations, inevitably the palace was still his destiny. In our lives, we will find ourselves in different places; whether it be a dark place, a place of transition, or a training place.

People may forget about us in the pit and the prison. In our dark and desolate place, the low and hard place, the place of trials and tribulation, the sick and broken places, and the barren and alone place, then just like the butler, remembrance shows up. God has a way of reminding us at just the right time.

Joseph, through God was able to interpret Pharaoh's dreams, the same man who threw him in the prison; the dungeon for a crime he did not even commit. My God! Be careful how you handle God's people. Be careful who you take advantage of, use, abuse, mistreat, manipulate, exploit, use intimidating tactics with, expose for selfish gain, who you do not value, because you never know when you may need him or her during this walk in Christ. You may wind up on the path with those you just double-crossed. You may have to suck up all pride and apologize. The pit is temporary, the prison is temporary, but the palace is destiny. We cannot give up in our temporary places. Like it is said, "the rainbow comes after the rain." Can you see the rainbow when it has not rained?

People won't always leave you during your pit or prison places, they may be by your side when you are going through for an ulterior motive. Some people mean you no good, and love to see you suffering and going through. They may look like they are suffering with you, when they are truly disguising themselves and cheering for your demise. Just like people can be around when you have it all, they can also be around when you are at your lowest to kick you even more. It can also be just the opposite. God has blessed you, His word has been manifested and they should be there cheering with you, but they are nowhere to be found. They were chanting for your expiration, but then God allowed you to birth new life in ministry, in finances, in health, whatever it is, and they could not stand it. "Can you stand to be blessed anyhow?" You will lose people along the way, but you have to be able to stand it.

As I faced the pit in my life, it was not an easy place, but it was a necessary place. The pit taught me how to appreciate the palace. The pit taught me how to pray for discernment and understanding. The pit could have become my destination were it not for the blood of Jesus.

If it were not for the blood of my Father, I could have died in the pit, but God! I could walk away from the pit knowing that "I am new creation in Christ Jesus, old things have passed away and behold all things have become new."

(Read 2 Corinthians 5:17)

One of my prison seasons was not too long ago, but I had to go by way of the prison to get my blessing. My God! I could have chosen to give up in between the four walls of the hospital, but I kept moving, kept pushing and believing that we shall live and not die. As each day passed between the walls of Palmetto Richland, I began to feel worthless and useless at a certain point. I couldn't really do much of anything besides lay and wait, but God had not forgotten about me even in that place. The fear of the unknown is debilitating. The uncertainty of what might happen would cross through my mind as I laid and waited. I was becoming a prisoner of my own thoughts. I had to get free! It began to feel like the walls were closing in on me and every day was growing longer and longer. I had to be strong for those that came to see me, but on the inside, I was ready to go. I wanted my baby to grow, be healthy, and arrive when she was supposed to. Regardless of the anguishing needles and every monitor or I.V. hooked up, every time I had to fast more than 24 hours, and having no water or food…my promise was the prize. Liberty was coming forth. Amen!

When you are used to having mobility and it is taken away and you can't do anything but just lie there and wait, it does something to you. I know we all say we would love to just rest and do nothing, but when you do not have a choice, "Oh, Jesus!" I want to take this time to thank a few people. First, I'd like to thank my Father, who chose me for this journey. He already knew everything that I could bear and that I would make it. I thank my husband for being by my side the entire time. He made sure home, our daughter and I, were taken care of and he still was running back and forth to work and to the hospital; preparing the house and our rooms for our return. I'd like to thank my baby girl, who came and stayed with me a few nights to keep me company. Thanks to my sister who came to stay with me a couple of nights from Georgia and my brother-in-law who came to visit. I am grateful for my mother-in-law and three sisters-in-law who came to visit with us from North Carolina. Much love to my parents who came to stay a week during my recovery process. I do not want to miss anybody so I won't start naming names, you know who you are that spent some quality time with me and prayed with me during my hospital stay. I appreciate each of you for taking time out of your busy schedules, plans to come and be a part of my story. It meant a lot. Your charity will not go unnoticed by God; He will reward you for your unselfish love.

Men and women of God please do not get discouraged in whatever place you are in right now. Just know that your home and destiny is the palace and you do not know defeat. You will make it. You will thrive. You will not only survive, but you shall live! Don't get stuck in the pit or the prison. Arrive to your destination and be a witness that God is good and that He finishes what He begins. God is very much alive and God will never leave you nor forsake you. Amen!.

WHAT CAN HINDER THE MOVE OF GOD
Chapter Twelve

As I look back over the things I've been through to include three pregnancies, I can tell you disobedience, stubbornness, and sin can hinder the move of God. When we are out of the will of God, we hinder His ability to move in our lives. When we make the choice to stay when God says move, we can hinder and block blessings in our lives. We can become upset with various things that come and go in our lives, but we must make the choice to forgive and move forward. When we choose to become rebellious, defiant, cruel, or fleshly, we stop walking out of the will of God and begin walking in our own will.

If we want God to move in our lives, we must free ourselves of the things that will hinder Him from fully operating. Other people aren't always the hindrance, rather it could be our pride, self-centered and self-righteousness that causes delay in our lives.

"What are you saying LaToya?" If we make the decision to be carnal about life challenges and that we have to respond to everything that comes in our direction, we make choices before consulting with the Father and we mess things up. We cannot choose the consequences that will not only affect our lives, but those connected to us when we put our hands on what belongs to God.

Not communing and praying can hinder God's movement in our lives. God could be waiting on you to come to Him and open your mouth, but you are too busy to give Him a few minutes out of your day. Your thought process is, "give me, give me, and give me." Well, it just doesn't work that way. You choose to hinder Him because you are too busy to spend time with Him. We then become idol worshippers, because we are putting other things ahead of Him and we know that is not His will for our lives.

Love can hinder the move of God. "How is our love walk? Do we love others as Christ love us or do we just give lip service?" We love one another in words, yet we don't speak to someone, we turn and walk another way when we see each other coming and we don't want to talk. We know someone needs a word of encouragement and we quench the spirit and turn away. "What kind of stuff is that?" We put love on the back burner and tell them a piece of our mind. We throw love in the trunk and come out the box on people. We are always talking about everybody, never loyal to anyone, but expect everyone to show us love. "What?" If our love is not right, it can hinder the move of God. Like the words says, *"And though I have the gift of prophecy, and understand all mysteries and all knowledge, and though I have all faith, so that I could remove mountains, but have not love, I am nothing." (1 Corinthians 13:2 NKJV)*

Division can hinder the move of God. We are not unified as one, we allow the enemy to cause havoc, chaos and confusion. Division opens the doors for discord, disharmony, and separation. "How can God move in all of that confusion?" We are praying one thing, but secretly complaining and not in alignment with anything. We say we are for one another, but as soon as opportunity opens up we will throw one another under a bus so quick it doesn't make any sense, but God! "How can God move when we are divided?" When you have everyone trying to lead and there are too many heads, that's another area of confusion and disorder. God is hindered when we are not unified.

Pride can hinder the move of God. When we think about Naaman; Elisha tells Naaman to go and wash in the dirty Jordan River. Elisha had not come out and greeted Naaman in the way he expected him to, and the healing was not even taking place the way that Naaman thought it should. Naaman knew that the rivers of Damascus coming out of the mountains as fresh streams, would be much better than the dirty Jordan River. We are all so sure that God could not possibly work through that group or in that way, so our spiritual pride continues to hinder a great work of God. God can move how and when He chooses because He is Sovereign. Therefore, we cannot allow pride to step in the way and think we know more than He does. Don't miss the move of God because we have allowed spiritual pride to creep in. Don't miss the move of God because God doesn't do it the way we think He should, or we think we are too good for the way He sent it. That's a trap that will keep you bound and sick.

Sin, yes, sin can hinder the move of God. We could be praying for a mighty move or change, but when we are habitually sinning, how can we expect God to move in our favor? *"...for all have sinned and fall short of the glory of God, being justified freely by His grace through the redemption that is in Christ Jesus..." (Romans 3:23-24).* We know that none is without sin, so we all have sinned and no one is righteous but One. No man is perfect, therefore we need Christ every day to make it. We could be asking for forgiveness over and over and still be living in sin and consciously repeating it. The Father will forgive us, but don't mock God. *"Do not be deceived, God is not mocked; for whatever a man sows, that he will also reap." Galatians 6:7*

I just want to encourage you that there are a lot of things that will hinder God moving in your life, so you need to examine your own life and seek the reason God may not be moving in a certain area. When you get into your secret place, I truly believe that God will reveal to you where that area is. Repent and get it right with God, so you can get out of that stuck place and move into the manifestation of all that He has for you.

The Push, The Pull and The Prayer…

The push that kept me going
The pull that grabbed my soul
The prayer that reached heaven
The pain no one would know

It was nothing that I had done
I just believed that I had won
He placed her in my spirit
He gave me her name too
Fasting, praying, and giving is what I had to do

I didn't know the tears that would come
I didn't know the pain I would face
I didn't know the time that would pass
All I knew is that God's word would last

God didn't work in my timing but His own
What He was doing in my life was unknown
It may have taken nine years to come true
But my God's love saw me through

The supernatural intervened in my womb
Created a new life and this life no tomb
He opened what was barren and He loosed what was bound
And a new precious life, what a beautiful sound

The push made me stronger
The pull got me through
The prayers that were lifted
Brought life to me and you too

We cannot give up
We cannot give in
But when we continue
Our destiny is to win
~ *LaToya Bilbo*

THE PUSH THE PULL AND THE PRAYER

I had to push through regardless of naysayers and haters, regardless of time, pressure, and what it looked like. In my waiting season, I still had to PUSH! We use the acronym as Pray Until Something Happens! When you are facing life storms, you must PUSH. When you feel like giving up, you must PUSH. When you think there is no hope, PUSH. There is a blessing in your pushing. The more you pray, the less room or access you give to the enemy to creep into your situation, into your life. Make a mental note or a visual picture in your mind. Every time you face something in life, see yourself physically pushing through.

I had to pull through the season by encouraging myself. With God's help I had to come out of what was clearly NOT the will of God for my life. I had to pull through seasons of disappointment, failure, hurt, pain, unhealthy relationships, doubt, setbacks and fear. Pulling through may not be easy. Pulling through may cause you to stretch and to drop some baggage off. Pulling through may cause you to lose some friends. Pulling through may cause you to get down on your knees more and open up your word to dig in. Your hunger and thirst is thriving when you pull through. You cannot stop at the PUSH, but you must continue to allow yourself to be PULLED by God through every situation and circumstance life throws at you.

I had to pray! Prayer was essential. Prayer changes things. There is no way that I would have made it through every place, every season in my life without prayer and communication with the Father. When I faced a difficult place or even when waiting just seemed too much, I had to pray. When I had to move out of my comfortable place into a transitional season, I had to pray. When I had to make some decisions, I had to pray. Prayer is essential as a believer. Jesus prayed. "Why do we think we can go day to day, week after week without prayer?" If it were not for prayer, I do not know where I would be right now. If I didn't have a personal relationship with God and communed with Him daily, I don't know how I could face my day.

We cannot live our lives lethargically, procrastinating, irresponsible, inconsistent, uncommitted, unaccountable, loveless, nasty, untruthful and expect God to move in our situations. This walk is not a punk walk. This walk is not for the weak. This walk is about more than us. Are we in it for the long haul or just for gifts and titles? We must be in it all the way to please God. God will supernaturally move in our situations when we are in tune with Him. He knows our desires. Our God wants us to live an abundant life and without faith, it's impossible to please God.

WAIT ON YOUR PROMISE
Chapter Thirteen

You may be questioning God right now about something you know He promised you but have yet to see it materialize. You have been praying, fasting, giving and staying the course. You have been persistent and committed but nothing. Things around you may be looking like, "it will never happen for me." Well I want to encourage you before I close out this book. I encourage you to change your thinking. When you start to think about the turn around, the promise, think positive. See it come to full fruition in your mindset, in your thoughts. You cannot allow the enemy to throw a smokescreen up in your thoughts. He will do whatever he can do to cause you doubt in God and your faith.

The devil does not mind us sitting in church every Sunday and Wednesday. The devil doesn't mind us singing in the choir or serving on the usher board. The devil doesn't even mind us standing before a crowd speaking a word. Man and woman of God when that word gets on the inside of us and we are not only hearers or readers but become DOERS of it; then the enemy has a problem.

The enemy knows you have a promise and his desire is to get you to doubt God and your faith. When you do this, you will begin to move out of the will of God. You begin to pray less, serve less, care less and become faithless. We must wait on our promise. Regardless of what it looks like, what people tell you or how tired you might have grown of waiting, wait. Praise Him while you wait. Rejoice in the wait. Learn in the wait. Growth will happen in your waiting process and when your promise comes, you will be ready for it. We always think we are ready for everything right away but we are not. God knows the exact hour, time and process for everything, so trust Him.

I want to encourage you today to wait on the promise. Do not give up on God because God will surely not give up on you. This is not just a cliché but its words to live by. God will never leave you nor forsake you. We give up on God and ourselves and think He has given up on us. It is not so. God's word will never return void and His word will set out to do everything it was spoken to do.

We have not because we do not ask or we ask amiss. It's time we line our thinking up with our speech. We can say a lot of things but our thinking can be the total opposite. We must believe what we say. We must say what we believe. Speak life and watch God turn your wait into something bigger than what you were ever expecting. There will be a testimony after this. Do you trust Him? Wait on your promise.

Many people throughout the Bible waited. Many people in your life have waited on things too. You are not the only one that has to wait. There are some things that happen quickly, immediately that we pray for, but then there are those things that we tarry for. Don't quit because it's taking too long. Keep pushing, pulling and praying; God is an on time God.

ENCOURAGEMENT AND CLOSING REMARKS:

Man and woman of destiny I just want to encourage you that the push may get rough, but keep on pushing. The pull may get hard, but keep on moving. Your prayers may seem that they are going amiss or taking forever to manifest, but you keep on praying, trusting and believing in God. God will come through. It may not be how we expect Him to answer, but you are His child and you belong to Him. God feeds the birds in the air, and makes sure the trees and lilies grow each year. God can heal sicknesses and diseases. God can cause a blind man to see. God can cause a deaf man to hear and the lame to walk.

God can open barren wombs and create life in something that is old.

God will truly deliver you, free you, heal you, prosper you, keep you, comfort you, make you new, make you fresh, cleanse you and withhold no good thing from you. In Him you lack nothing, regardless of what it looks like in the natural, you lack nothing!

I encourage you to think about the last time God did something for you. I encourage you to think about someone who didn't make it this morning, yesterday, last week, last year. I encourage you to think about how many days you have gone without food, drink, clothing, shelter, transportation, finances and more. We have so much to be grateful and thankful for. We are living in a country that is turning its back on the things of God. We cannot go astray with man's laws, but we must keep moving forward in the things of the Kingdom. Regardless of what the world legislates and says is okay, we must stand on the word of God. His words will be the last thing standing when it's all said and done. Man may not bow to Him now, but there will come a time that all men will bow and worship Him. Why not choose to worship Him in spirit and truth, now? Don't let distractions by what you see the world worshipping and idolizing. You serve an awesome God!

In closing, I pray that although the push, the pull, and the prayer related to my personal trials, tribulations, and testimonies of pregnancies that anyone reading this was able to receive a word from above. Even if it was just one word, I pray that you will meditate on it and get all that God has for you in this time. You are vital! You are valuable! Don't give up on God because He will not give up on you. Please continue to keep my family and me in your prayers as I do the same for you. I may not know you by name or even face, but guess what, God does. I am praying for all God's people. I love you and pray and hope that none perish and spend eternity in hell. I am looking to see you in my Father's house. Amen!

www.ingramcontent.com/pod-product-compliance
Lightning Source LLC
LaVergne TN
LVHW041236080426
835508LV00011B/1230